I've Been Arrested...Now What?

A Simple Look At What To Expect

Federal Criminal Process

**By John Michael Crim
A Former Federal Inmate**

First Printing
February 2014
ISBN-13: 978-1495924835
JohnCrim@mail.com

Table of Contents

Introduction	1
Why Am I Here?	4
The Indictment (18 USC §3361)	
Held as a Material Witness	
A Co-Defendant Testifying Against You	
What Will Happen To Me?	6
Attorney Representation	
Arraignment, Entering The Plea (18 USC §3433)	
Making Bail	
Plea Agreement (18 USC §3438)	
Speedy Trial Act, The Trial (18 USC §3161)	
Sentencing (18 USC §3551, seq.)	
Designation To A Prison (18 USC §3621)	

How Much Time Am I Facing?	12
Sentencing Guidelines (U.S.S.G.)	
Downward/Upward Departure & The PSI	
Statutes of Limitation	
Substantial Assistance (U.S.S.G. §5K1.1)	
Should I Go To Trial?	16
You Could Get More Time	
Is My Attorney Competent? Communicate?	
Did I Make Bail	
It's Not As Bad As The Government Leads You To Believe	18
Government Threats	
Issues That May Reduce My Prison Time	
BOP/Congressional Benefits	20
Drug Program & Time Off (RDAP)(18 USC §3624(e))	
Good Conduct Time Off (18 USC §3624(b))	

Halfway House (RRC)(18 USC §3624(c)(2))	
Home Confinement (18 USC §3624(c)(2))	
Skills Development System (42 USC §17541(a)(1)(G))	
Change In The Law	
Progressing To A Lower Security Level Prison	
Letter From Director Of The Bureau Of Prisons	**25**
Sentencing Table	**26**

Introduction

The nature of the U.S. plea bargain system had been repellant to me for many years, and I was, as in so many other related matters, about to receive a bruising practical education in it. It is the exchange of testimony for varied sentences. It generally starts well down in an organization and brings irresistible pressures to bear on people unable to sustain themselves psychologically or defend themselves financially against such an onslaught – until that person promises to inculpate (tell on) a higher-up.

The process goes through an organization until sometimes scores of intimidated or suborned people are accusing the chosen target. It is an evil and profoundly corrupt process. It is not reconcilable with traditional American notions of the law. Every informed person in the country knows that the criminal justice system is based on officially sanctioned fraud and intimidation that the courthouses are silent and the courts empty because almost no one can go the distance with the government, and accusations that are extorted. But almost no one says anything about it.

"A Matter of Principle" – Author Conrad Black

This Pamphlet was produced out of necessity, as the author had witnessed far too many injustices in the U.S. legal system, preying on the illiterate and unknowledgeable person. Hopefully you will see this information as easy reading and understanding.

Please Distribute This Pamphlet

It is the wish of the author that this publication gets reprinted (by whatever source possible) and widely distributed to all new detainees who find themselves as a target of the U.S. government.

Why Am I Here?

The Indictment
18 USC, §3361

In order for the government to prosecute a person, they must do one of two things:

1. Prosecutor must obtain permission (indictment) from the Federal Grand Jury. This is the formal charging document (accusation) that shows the U.S. Code(s) that you have been accused of violating. You must look this Code up and see what the exact wording is, as well as the penalty (a true bill); or

2. Prosecutor must bring an accusation in writing, signed under oath of office, informing you of the charge(s). No indictment needed.

Held As A Material Witness

Sometimes a person is detained because they have valuable information that will assist the government in prosecuting some other person. Charges might not be against you.

A Co-Defendant Testifying Against You In a multi-person indictment, the government may offer (proffer) you a plea deal in exchange for your testimony against another person. This is known as a §5K1.1 downward departure in your sentence. Usually the first to make a deal will receive this benefit. You would then be obligated to assist the government in prosecuting other persons, even in other cases. The court must inform the jury that this witness's testimony was in exchange for a reduction in his/her sentence (if there is a trial).

What Will Happen To Me?

Attorney Representation

After the accusation is made against you, you will retain (pay for) an attorney, or have the court appoint one if you can't afford one. The attorney is to act on your behalf, and no one can contact (question) you without this attorney's presence. (This means the prosecutor, agents, and other attorneys). In fact, your attorney should advise you to not speak to anyone other than him/her. Your attorney must provide competent and effective assistance in your defense. The attorney must advise you:

1. YOUR RIGHT TO A SPEEDY TRIAL (70 DAYS)
2. YOUR RIGHT TO HAVE AN ATTORNEY FOR EVERY STAGE OF YOUR CRIMINAL CASE
3. HOW MUCH TIME YOU ARE FACING
4. YOUR RIGHT TO ASK FOR BAIL
5. ANY OTHER PUNISHMENT OR CONSEQUENCES

Arraignment, Entering The Plea
18 USC, §3361

The first stage is the arraignment. You will be brought in front of the judge. The judge will explain the charge(s) against you, and ask it your attorney has explained this to you. The judge will ask you how you plea to the charge(s) (i.e guilty, not guilty, or nolo contendere). The issue of bail may be raised, or another court date is set.

Making Bail You will have a bail hearing in which the judge will set the amount and condition of bail. The prosecutor can object or agree to it. In the federal system most bail requires property to be put up to cover the set amount of bail. Once the government confirms that the pledged property is not liened, the probation office will process your release. Don't ever fail to show up to court appointments, otherwise you will not qualify for Camp (minimum security facility), and may forfeit the pledged property. Expect the process to take some time. If you can't make bail, you will remain in the detention center until you are acquitted at trial or designated to a prison to serve your sentence.

Plea Agreement If you choose to enter
18 USC, §3438   into a plea agreement with the government, you should consider many things. There are different types of pleas. The judge is not bound by the agreement between you and the government. So it is advisable to

make sure the agreement states that you can withdraw it if the judge goes beyond what you have agreed to. Your attorney must competently advise you about the terms of the agreement. (See Strickland v. Washington, 466 U.S. 668, 80 L.Ed.2d 674) The government will include terms that you have agreed to waive your right to a trial, appeals, habeas relief, and possibly waive any right to have your sentence reduced if a law changes in your favor.

The prosecutor enjoys putting pressure on you to hurry and make a decision. However, don't fall for this; the prosecutor does not want to go to trial any more than you. There are only so many cases that can proceed to court in a day. Demand that your attorney make a counter-offer (if you are in a position to do so) for something that you can live with. Many defendants have been able to enter an agreement on the day of trial, or even during the trial. Remember, the judge has the decision of accepting or rejecting your plea.

The U.S. Supreme Court has said that if you enter a guilty plea with the government, the promises and inducements must be fulfilled. (See Santobello v. N.Y., 404 U.S. 257, 262, 30 L.Ed.2d 427, 433) The government cannot breach a plea agreement because it decided after the fact that it has made a bad bargain. The judge cannot participate in the negotiations of a plea. Your attorney is obligated to tell you about everything that effects your decision to enter a plea. You cannot be punished for a firearm charge if you did not agree to it in your plea agreement (or found guilty of it by a jury). (See Alleyne v. U.S., 133 S.Ct. 2151 (2013))

Speedy Trial Act
18 USC, §3161

Once you have entered your final plea of not guilty with the government and the court, the government has 70 days in which to bring you to trial. The exceptions to this are, if the court decides the case to be "complex", and/or a defendant files any pre-trial motion that requires an answer from the government.

If you are proceeding to trial, your attorney should be competent and experienced enough to know when to make objections in order to preserve the issue for appeal. This may mean that he/she needs to object to evidence, testimony, or findings by the judge. He/she may also need to object to a quantity amount of drug or monetary loss, as well as whether it is attributable to you. He/she may request an acquittal on a count which has insufficient evidence to support a conviction. If you want to appeal the case, you need to make it known at the end of trial (or within 10 days of the judgment). Which means that you need to make the request with the judge if it seems your attorney doesn't want to do an appeal. You have the right to appeal if you went to trial and some error was made. You will be sentenced at a later date, as much as 4-6 months later. If motions are filed after trial, but before sentencing, it could delay sentencing.

Sentencing
18 USC, §3551, seq

The sentencing is one of the most important stages in your case. So, your attorney should spend enough time in addressing issues (in a sentencing memorandum) regarding your punishment. Does your attorney understand the Sentencing Guidelines? Does he/she understand "grouping" the counts, and whether the counts should runn consecutive or concurrently? Does he/she know if you are eligible for any downward departures, safety valve, and acceptance of responsibility? Make sure that you request the court to recommend that you be designated to a specific area for serving your prison term, and recommend the RDAP program if you have a drug-related case. The level of security will determine what prison you will be designated to (USP,

Medium, Low, or Minimum). So, you will need to ask the judge if you can self-surrender at the prison. It is worth a 3-level reduction in your security score.

Designation To A Prison
18 USC, §3621

When considering where you want to do your time, you might want to consider the following:

1. Is it near (within 500 miles) my family?

2. Is the prison run by the BOP or a contractor?

3. Is it large enough to offer vocational education programs?

4. Does it have the RDAP program?

The designation process will take about 4-5 weeks to complete. Then you will be taken out of the detention center and transported to the prison (if you are still in the center). If you are allowed to self-surrender, the judge will notify you as to the date and location.

How Much Time Am I Facing?

The punishment stage utilizes many factors in determining how much time you serve in prison, how much time you serve under probation (supervised Release), hoe much time you get off, restitution and fine.

Sentencing Guidelines
U.S.S.G.

The U.S. Sentencing Commission is responsible for setting out the guidelines for punishment. They may from time to time modify those statutes. You may be eligible to take advantage of those changes it they are made to take effect retroactively to when you were sentenced. In 2005, the U.S. Supreme Court in U.S. v. Booker, 543 U.S. 220, 160 L.Ed.2d 621, ruled that the U.S. Sentencing Guidelines are only advisory. This means that the judge and probation office will use the guidelines as a starting point, and then use their own judgment to finalize a sentence computation.

Downward/ Upward Departure & PSI

The Probation office will prepare a Presentence Investigation Report (PSI) that will be served on all parties ten days prior to the sentencing date. See 18 USC §3552(d). Objections to the PSI should be made soon after that. It is very important that the PSI be accurate. If you have objections, you need to have those made as an attachment to the PSI. The PSI will have details of your background, character, prior convictions, and a computation of your offense level and Criminal history Category. It starts with a base offense level that is based solely on the statute you were found guilty of. Then it will show any recommendations for upward and downward departures such as supervisory role, more than five victims, monetary loss amount, sophisticated means, and anything that is considered yo have aggravated the criminal activity. Downward departures can reduce your length of sentence, which may consist of acceptance of responsibility, paying back losses to victims prior to trial, minimal role, substantial assistance to the government, showing remorse, and any factor that overly states the seriousness of the offense. Your attorney should file a sentencing memorandum five to seven days prior to sentencing. Statistics show that in 80% of the cases, judges come to the bench with their minds made up as to what sentence they will impose. The memorandum is your opportunity to explain in more detail what you believe the sentence should be. If you want the RDAP program, it is very important that you don't understate (or play down) your substance abuse.

Statutes Of Limitation

Many statutes that are under the criminal code have limits in which you can be sentenced to. For example: 18 USC, §371 is the conspiracy to defraud the U.S. statute which carries a maximum sentence of 60 months. Some statutes have a mandatory minimum in which the judge must sentence you to. For example: 18 USC, §924(c)(1) is a firearm statute, which if charged along with a drug offense, carries a minimum sentence of 60 months, and must run consecutive to the drug charge. Some statutes have a time requirement in which the government must bring the charge against you. For example: 26 USC, §7203 is for willful failure to file a tax return, or pay the tax. This statute carries a maximum of one year in prison, and must be brought against you within three years of when the return was due. If the government has failed to follow these statutes, your attorney would need to move for dismissal of the charge.

Substantial Assistance

U.S.S.G., §5K1.1

The U.S. Sentencing Guidelines statutes provide for a reduction in your sentence if you provided substantial assistance to the government. This is know as a §5K1.1 reduction, and the prosecutor must move the court, under Rule 35(b), in order for you to get the reduction. When you make an agreement with the government to provide substantial assistance, you are obligated to testify for the government in any case; yours and any other case they request. If the prosecutor feels that your testimony or information is not helpful, they can refuse to move the court for a reduction.

Should I Go To Trial?

You Could Get More Time

The reason for plea agreement is to assure that you will receive a lower sentence so it is to your advantage to enter a plea agreement if the evidence points to your guilt. It is also to the government's advantage because they won't be going through a lengthy and expensive trial. However, if you know that you are innocent, and the government has no evidence to convict you, you should exercise your right to a jury trial. Keep in mind that if you make the government go to trial, and you lose, the government will seek the maximum penalty that is provided by law. This is often much greater than the penalty the government offered you in the plea negotiations. Make sure your attorney gives you competent advice.

Is My Attorney Competent?

A very important issue to consider when thinking about going to trial is, does my attorney have the competence and experience to conduct an effective defense on my behalf. If you are not familiar with the law and the criminal process, you may not know if your attorney is doing a good or bad job. One way to know if the attorney is competent is whether he/she is willing to communicate with you. The attorney has the right to not take into consideration your legal theories; however, he/she must communicate with you. The attorney should be asking you a lot of questions about your alleged crime. The attorney also meeds to interview potential defense witnesses, as well as examine all the evidence. Another issue to consider is, does my attorney do appeals (if that is available to you)? It is best to have the same attorney to handle all stages of your case. Don't be afraid to ask the attorney what his/her success record is with trials (how many cases like yours?).

Did I Make Bail? When considering whether to go to trial, you may tend to want to get it over with and enter a plea agreement just so you will spend less time in prison. However, when you are on bail, you will have no such pressure, and tend to want to go to trial. So, don't let the fact that you are in the detention center be the reason to not go to trial. Of course, you may be eligible for bail once you enter into the plea agreement, which makes the issue of going to trial moot.

It's Not As Bad As The Government Leads You To Believe

Government Threats Being in the detention center is the worst place to be when trying to decide what to do. The prosecutor knows this and will use it to his/her advantage. The prosecutor will come to you with a plea deal and say that it is only good during that meeting, and will expire when you leave the meeting with them. The prosecutor has also been known to use family and friends as a weapon. They are good at telling you that they will prosecute someone like this to try and get you to break down and "save" your family from being charged. Some of this may be empty threats, and some may not. You need to decide what chances are of a family member being charged and convicted. The prosecutor is also good at overstating the facts of the case. For example: you might be told that you will be facing 140 years if you don't cooperate with the government. I know for a fact that this happened and the guy committed suicide. You may even be told that you will not receive any downward departure unless you cooperate. Remember, the judge is the only one who you need to be concerned with, because he/she is the only who makes that decision. The prosecutor and the Probation Office simply give recommendations to the judge, and those are often times different than what is told to you in the negotiations of a plea deal.

Issues That May Reduce my Prison Time

There are issues that may reduce your prison time that the prosecutor will not tell you, in fact, your own attorney may not tell you. These are more fully explained in the nest section. So, keep in mind that things are not always what they seem to be. This is a fight in which the government will use what they can in order to pressure you.

BOP/Congressional Benefits

Drug Program & Time Off
18 USC, §3624(e)

The BOP offers a drug abuse treatment program to help prepare you for release and help you cope with your addiction. Almost every prison in the BOP offers a 40-hour "non-residential" drug treatment program, drug education program, Narcotics Anonymous and Alcoholics Anonymous groups, and individual counseling. However, there are thirty or so prisons in the BOP which offer the 500-hour "residential" drug abuse treatment program (RDAP), which is designed to intensively counsel inmates regarding drug abuse issues. The 500-hour drug and alcohol abuse treatment program is nine months long and is usually found at medium-security, low-security and minimum-security prisons. When inmates are 90% of the way to their §3624(e) release date (full sentence less good conduct time, less reduction of successful completion of the RDAP in and outpatient program), they are eligible for referral to home confinement. Under the incentive, some will be eligible for early release benefit of up to 12 months (the BOP average is 8.5 months) and an extended halfway house and home confinement placement (usually six months) at the end of their sentence. Remember, your PSI report must include detailed history of your drug and/or alcohol abuse. It is also helpful if you participate in community-based substance abuse treatment within the 12 months prior to your incarceration (even while out on bail).

Good Conduct Time Off
18 USC, §3624(b)

Congress has provided an incentive for inmates who have conducted themselves in a good manner (without serious incident). The statute provides for the BOP to grant time off of your sentence of up to 54 days for each year served in custody. The average is 47 days, and has been upheld by the Supreme Court as a discretion belonging to the BOP. This time off is not vested until your release date. See BOP Program Statement 5880.28(3)(g).

Halfway House
18 USC, §3624(c)(2)

Congress has provided an incentive for inmates to spend up to 12 months of the last part of their sentence in a Residential Re-entry Center (RRC) or otherwise known as a halfway house. This is for the purpose of searching for employment and a place to live. It is a way to re-enter the community in a progressive and controlled environment.

Home Confinement
18 USC, §3624(c)(2)

Congress has provided an incentive for inmates to spend up to six months of the end of your sentence at home confinement, or ten percent of your sentence, whichever is less, at home confinement. The purpose here is for those who already have a source of income and a place to live and need to slowly re-enter the community.

Skills Development
42 USC §17541(a)(1)(G)

The BOP implemented a new automated, web-based assessment and tracking tool to help staff identify inmates' strengths and weaknesses, entitled the Inmate Skills Development System (ISDS). Information is gathered from a variety of sources, including court documents and behavioral observations, and entered at the time of initial classification. The computerized program assists in establishing identifiable skill deficits and offering programs to the inmate to reduce these deficits. The incentive for bettering oneself is release to the halfway house early.

Changes In The Law

The law (statute) that you were convicted of might change after sentencing. This includes the Sentencing Guidelines. If that change was made to apply retroactively, you may file a motion (or the public defender) in the court for a reduction of your sentence. For example: on November 1, 2011, the guidelines changed that affected the quantity amount of crack cocaine it would take to reach a specific offense level (was 100:1 ratio between crack and powder cocaine; now 18:1). This could effectively lower your level by 4 offense levels. You would have one year to take advantage of the change in the law. Make sure that your plea agreement does not waive this right. The government tries to include terms in the agreement that best favors them. There are other ways that a change in the law can benefit you. The amount of Good Conduct Time could increase. The crack cocaine ratio could change from 18:1 to 1:1.

Progressing to a Lower Security Level Prison

Just because you are initially classified to a certain prison security level, it does not mean you will stay at that level. A security level is high because of a number of reasons. For example: young age, time remaining to serve, threat to the community, incident reports (disciplinary), or nature of offense. As your security level decreases, you may qualify for a lower security level prison.

THE
INNOCENT
MAN

LETTER FROM DIRECTOR OF THE BUREAU OF PRISONS

U. S. Department of Justice

Federal Bureau of Prisons

Office of the Director *Washington DC 20534*

July 23, 2012

MEMORANDUM FOR ALL INMATES

FROM: Charles E. Samuels, Jr., Director

SUBJECT: Suicide Prevention

As Director of the Federal Bureau of Prisons, I am committed to ensuring your safety, the safety of staff and the public. In this message, I would like to specifically address your state of mind, an important part of your overall well-being.

Incarceration is difficult for many people; many individuals experience a wide range of emotions - sadness, anxiety, fear, loneliness, anger, or shame. At times you may feel hopeless about your future and your thoughts may turn to suicide. If you are unable to think of solutions other than suicide, it is not because solutions do not exist; it is because you are currently unable to see them. Do not lose hope. Solutions can be found, feelings change, unanticipated positive events occur. Look for meaning and purpose in educational and treatment programs, faith, work, family, and friends.

Staff are a key resource available to you. The Bureau's contracts with private providers require contractors to have mental health professionals who provide counseling and other supportive mental health services. Anytime you want to speak with a mental health professional, let staff know and they will make the necessary arrangements. Your unit officer, unit team, work supervisor, and teachers are available to speak with you and provide assistance as are other staff in the institution. Help is available.

Each day, inmates across the country find the strength and support to move ahead in a positive direction, despite their challenging circumstances. You may be reading this letter while in a Special Housing Unit cell, thinking your life is moving in the wrong direction. But wherever you are, whatever your circumstances, my commitment to you is the same. I want you to succeed. I want your life to go forward in a positive direction - a direction personally fulfilling to you, but also a direction which ensures the safety of the staff and inmates who interact with you each day.

I know your road ahead is not an easy one. Be willing to request help from those around you.

"Learn from yesterday, live for today, hope for tomorrow." - Albert Einstein

SENTENCING TABLE

(in months of imprisonment)

	Offense Level	Criminal History Category (Criminal History Points)					
		I (0 or 1)	II (2 or 3)	III (4, 5, 6)	IV (7, 8, 9)	V (10, 11, 12)	VI (13 or more)
	1	0-6	0-6	0-6	0-6	0-6	0-6
	2	0-6	0-6	0-6	0-6	0-6	1-7
	3	0-6	0-6	0-6	0-6	2-8	3-9
	4	0-6	0-6	0-6	2-8	4-10	6-12
Zone A	5	0-6	0-6	1-7	4-10	6-12	9-15
	6	0-6	1-7	2-8	6-12	9-15	12-18
	7	0-6	2-8	4-10	8-14	12-18	15-21
	8	0-6	4-10	6-12	10-16	15-21	18-24
	9	4-10	6-12	8-14	12-18	18-24	21-27
Zone B	10	6-12	8-14	10-16	15-21	21-27	24-30
	11	8-14	10-16	12-18	18-24	24-30	27-33
Zone C	12	10-16	12-18	15-21	21-27	27-33	30-37
	13	12-18	15-21	18-24	24-30	30-37	33-41
	14	15-21	18-24	21-27	27-33	33-41	37-46
Zone D	15	18-24	21-27	24-30	30-37	37-46	41-51
	16	21-27	24-30	27-33	33-41	41-51	46-57
	17	24-	27-	30-	37-	46-	51-63

	30	33	37	46	57	
18	27-33	30-37	33-41	41-51	51-63	57-71
19	30-37	33-41	37-46	46-57	57-71	63-78
20	33-41	37-46	41-51	51-63	63-78	70-87
21	37-46	41-51	46-57	57-71	70-87	77-96
22	41-51	46-57	51-63	63-78	77-96	84-105
23	46-57	51-63	57-71	70-87	84-105	92-115
24	51-63	57-71	63-78	77-96	92-115	100-125
25	57-71	63-78	70-87	84-105	100-125	110-137
26	63-78	70-87	78-97	92-115	110-137	120-150
27	70-87	78-97	87-108	100-125	120-150	130-162
28	78-97	87-108	97-121	110-137	130-162	140-175
29	87-108	97-121	108-135	121-151	140-175	151-188
30	97-121	108-135	121-151	135-168	151-188	168-210
31	108-135	121-151	135-168	151-188	168-210	188-235
32	121-151	135-168	151-188	168-210	188-235	210-262
33	135-168	151-188	168-210	188-235	210-262	235-293
34	151-188	168-210	188-235	210-262	235-293	262-327
35	168-210	188-235	210-262	235-293	262-327	292-365
36	188-235	210-262	235-293	262-327	292-365	324-405
37	210-262	235-293	262-327	292-365	324-405	360-life

	I	II	III	IV	V	VI
38	235-293	262-327	292-365	324-405	360-life	360-life
39	262-327	292-365	324-405	360-life	360-life	360-life
40	292-365	324-405	360-life	360-life	360-life	360-life
41	324-405	360-life	360-life	360-life	360-life	360-life
42	360-life	360-life	360-life	360-life	360-life	360-life
43	life	life	life	life	life	life

Commentary to Sentencing Table

Application Notes:

1. The Offense Level (1-43) forms the vertical axis of the Sentencing Table. The Criminal History Category (I-VI) forms the horizontal axis of the Table. The intersection of the Offense Level and Criminal History Category displays the Guideline Range in months of imprisonment. "Life" means life imprisonment. For example, the guideline range applicable to a defendant with an Offense Level of 15 and a Criminal History Category of III is 24-30 months of imprisonment.

2. In rare cases, a total offense level of less than 1 or more than 43 may result from application of the guidelines. A total offense level of less than 1 is to be treated as an offense level of 1. An offense level of more than 43 is to be treated as an offense level of 43.

3. The Criminal History Category is determined by the total criminal history points from Chapter Four, Part A, except as provided in §§4B1.1 (Career Offender) and 4B1.4 (Armed Career Criminal). The total criminal history points associated with each Criminal History Category are shown under each Criminal History Category in the Sentencing Table.

www.ingramcontent.com/pod-product-compliance
Lightning Source LLC
Chambersburg PA
CBHW051826170526
45167CB00005B/2177